PIANO

Adventures® *by Nancy and Randall Faber*

_____ is sightreading this book!

(your name)

Production Coordinator: Jon Ophoff
Cover: Terpstra Design, San Francisco
Illustrations: Erika LeBarre

ISBN 978-1-61677-671-8
Copyright © 2015 Dovetree Productions, Inc.
c/o FABER PIANO ADVENTURES, 3042 Creek Dr., Ann Arbor, MI 48108.
International Copyright Secured. All Rights Reserved. Printed in U.S.A.
WARNING: The music, text, design, and graphics in this publication are protected
by copyright law. Any duplication is an infringement of U.S. copyright law.

CHART YOUR PROGRESS

Sightreading for Lesson Book 3A, pp. 6–7
Sakura... 6–9

☐ DAY 1 ☐ DAY 2 ☐ DAY 3 ☐ DAY 4 ☐ DAY 5

Sightreading for Lesson Book 3A, pp. 24–25
Lunar Eclipse 30–33

☐ DAY 1 ☐ DAY 2 ☐ DAY 3 ☐ DAY 4 ☐ DAY 5

Sightreading for Lesson Book 3A, pp. 12–13
Looking-Glass River.....................10–13

☐ DAY 1 ☐ DAY 2 ☐ DAY 3 ☐ DAY 4 ☐ DAY 5

Sightreading for Lesson Book 3A, p. 27
Scarborough Fair......................... 34–37

☐ DAY 1 ☐ DAY 2 ☐ DAY 3 ☐ DAY 4 ☐ DAY 5

Sightreading for Lesson Book 3A, pp. 14–15
Yellow Bird 14–17

☐ DAY 1 ☐ DAY 2 ☐ DAY 3 ☐ DAY 4 ☐ DAY 5

Sightreading for Lesson Book 3A, pp. 32–33
Night of the Tarantella 38–43

☐ DAY 1 ☐ DAY 2 ☐ DAY 3 ☐ DAY 4 ☐ DAY 5

Sightreading for Lesson Book 3A, pp. 16–17
Morning 18–21

☐ DAY 1 ☐ DAY 2 ☐ DAY 3 ☐ DAY 4 ☐ DAY 5

Sightreading for Lesson Book 3A, pp. 34–35
Candles and Cake........................ 44–47

☐ DAY 1 ☐ DAY 2 ☐ DAY 3 ☐ DAY 4 ☐ DAY 5

Sightreading for Lesson Book 3A, pp. 20–21
Land of the Silver Birch 22–25

☐ DAY 1 ☐ DAY 2 ☐ DAY 3 ☐ DAY 4 ☐ DAY 5

Sightreading for Lesson Book 3A, pp. 36–37
Amazing Grace 48–51

☐ DAY 1 ☐ DAY 2 ☐ DAY 3 ☐ DAY 4 ☐ DAY 5

Sightreading for Lesson Book 3A, pp. 22–23
Cossack Ride 26–29

☐ DAY 1 ☐ DAY 2 ☐ DAY 3 ☐ DAY 4 ☐ DAY 5

Sightreading for Lesson Book 3A, p. 39
March Slav................................... 52–55

☐ DAY 1 ☐ DAY 2 ☐ DAY 3 ☐ DAY 4 ☐ DAY 5

SIGHTREADING SKILL

Sightreading skill is a powerful asset for the developing pianist. It makes every step of music-making easier. With the right tools and a little effort, sightreading skill can be developed to great benefit.

This book builds confident, early-intermediate sightreaders in these ways:

1. Facile recognition of **notes** and **intervals**, including **ledger lines**.

2. Perception of common **rhythmic patterns** in $\frac{4}{4}$, $\frac{3}{4}$, $\frac{3}{8}$, and $\frac{6}{8}$.

3. Recognition of key signatures with an understanding of tonality; tonic, dominant, leading tone, and primary chords I-IV-V7 (or i-iv-V7).

Music reading involves more than a sequence of note names. The sightreader tracks *horizontally* and *vertically*, observing melodic and harmonic intervals, chords, rhythmic and melodic motives, dynamics, and accompaniment patterns that make up the context of the music.

This decoding skill requires repetition within familiar musical frameworks. In other words, pattern recognition develops by seeing a lot of the same patterns. Accordingly, this book presents **musical variations** to sharpen perception of the *new* against a backdrop of the *familiar*. More than any other instrumentalist, the pianist must group notes into patterns for musical understanding.

In the Level 3A Sightreading Book, these musical variations are drawn from the music introduced in the 3A Lesson Book—traditional folk songs, jazz styles, Faber originals, and classic themes by Hook, Grieg, and Tchaikovsky.

The book features the keys of C, G, F, and D, with their scales and primary chords, along with triplets and one-octave arpeggios.

Get ready for a 3A Sightreading Adventure!

SIGHTREADING

How to Use

This book is organized into sets of 5 exercises for 5 days of practice. Each set provides variations on a piece from the Piano Adventures® Level 3A Lesson Book. Play one exercise a day, completing one set per week.

Though the student is not required to repeatedly "practice" the sightreading exercise, each should be repeated as indicated by the repeat sign. For an extra workout, play each of the previous exercises in the set before playing the new exercise of the day.

Curiosity and Fun

The "Don't Practice This!" motto is a bold statement which has an obvious psychological impact. It reminds us that sightreading is indeed the first time through and it reminds us to keep the activity fun.

Level of Difficulty

It is most beneficial to sightread at the appropriate level of difficulty. By setting a slow, steady tempo, the student should be able to play the majority of the notes, especially on the repetition. This Piano Adventures® Sightreading Book is carefully written to provide an appropriate challenge for the Level 3A student.

Marking Progress

In previous levels, students were encouraged to draw a large **X** over each completed exercise. Due to the higher level of the student, this is now optional.

Some students may exclaim about the thickness of the book. They soon are rewarded to find how fast they can move through it. Indeed, with confidence increasing, the student can take pride in moving to completion of this very large book ... and do so with a crescendo of achievement.

Instructions to the Student

1. **Always scan the music before playing.**
   This strategy helps you "take in" the music you will be sightreading.
   You will get better and faster at "scanning" with experience.

2. **Scan the basics first.**

   - What is the key?

   - What is the time signature?

   - What measures look difficult? Mentally hear them before playing.
     You may wish to tap the rhythm lightly in your lap.

   - Now look for patterns. Are there any measures that repeat? How many?

   - Can you spot I, IV, or V7 chords?

   - Scan for scale passages and thumb-crossings. Any hand shifts?

   - Now scan for dynamics, sharps, flats, naturals, and rests.

3. **Count-off the tempo.**

   - Set a slow, steady tempo of two measures. Keep your eyes moving ahead as you play! Repeat the exercise.

   - You may wish to put a big X through the music to show completion.

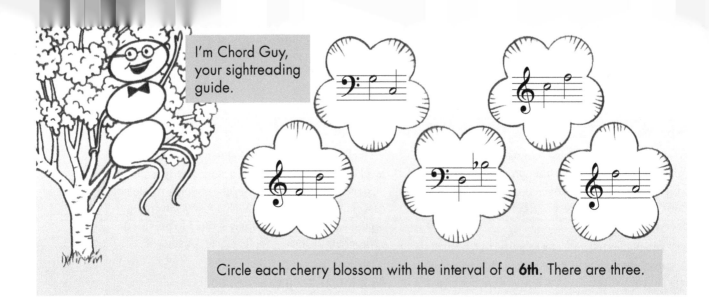

I'm Chord Guy, your sightreading guide.

Circle each cherry blossom with the interval of a **6th**. There are three.

DAY 1: Sakura

DON'T PRACTICE THIS!

Scan the music. Do you see an 8th-note rhythm pattern?

DAY 2: Sakura

Where is there an echo in this piece?

DAY 3: Sakura

Plan the R.H. shift from measure 2 to measure 3 before you play.

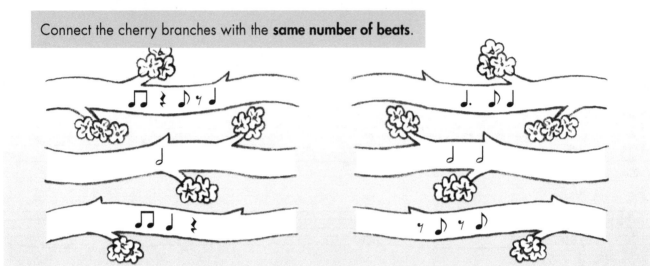

Connect the cherry branches with the **same number of beats**.

DAY 4: Sakura

Notice the dynamic contrast from *forte* to *piano* in the music.

DON'T
PRACTICE
THIS!

DAY 5: Sakura

(for L.H. alone)

Scan the pedaling before playing.

DON'T PRACTICE THIS!

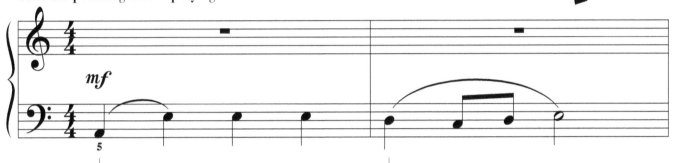

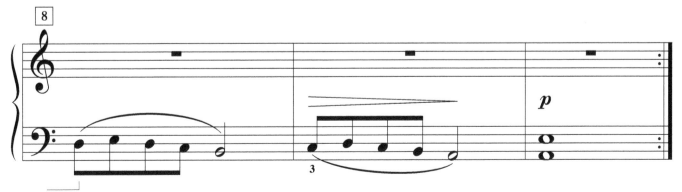

DAY 1: Looking-Glass River

Key of _____ Major

Silently finger the R.H. ascending and descending scales before playing.

Circle the two correct **Alberti bass** patterns.
Remember: bottom-top-middle-top.

DAY 2: Looking-Glass River
Key of _____ Major

What interval does the R.H. play throughout?

DAY 3: Looking-Glass River
Key of _____ Major

Scan the L.H. Alberti bass. Where do you change to the IV chord?

DAY 4: Looking-Glass River

Key of _____ Major

DON'T PRACTICE THIS!

The L.H. Alberti bass pattern uses the I, IV, and V7 chords.
Plan how you will play each.

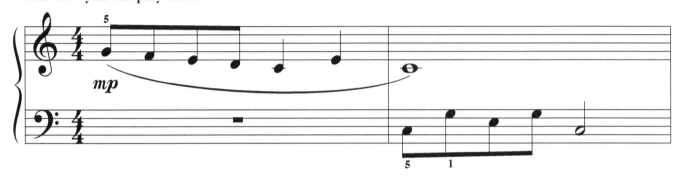

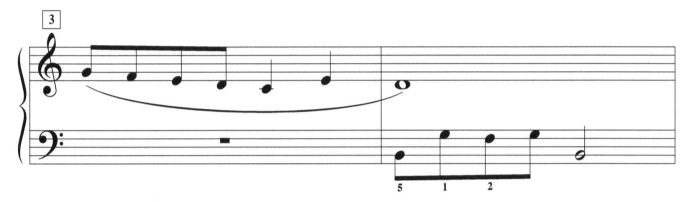

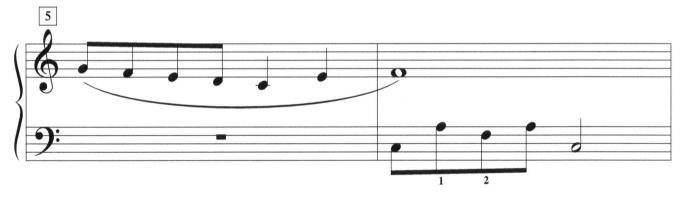

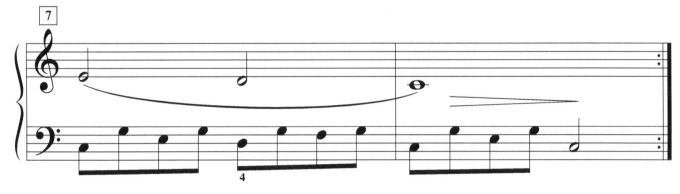

Well done, sightreader!
Name each note in the blanks.

_ O N _ R _ T U L _ T I O N S

DAY 5: Looking-Glass River

Key of _____ Major

DON'T PRACTICE THIS!

Scan the R.H. notes. Silently finger the interval at measure 3.
Silently finger the scale at measure 7.

13

Draw **bar lines** for the rhythm above.

DAY 1: Yellow Bird

Key of _____ Major

Plan how you will play the rhythm at measure 2.
Is this a rhythm pattern that occurs again?

DON'T
PRACTICE
THIS!

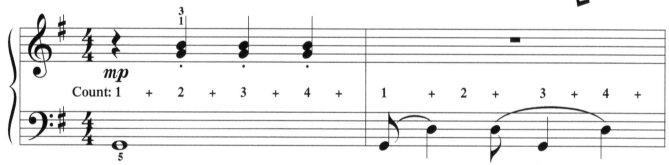

Count: 1 + 2 + 3 + 4 + 1 + 2 + 3 + 4 +

DAY 2: Yellow Bird

Key of _____ Major

Be sure to notice the key signature!

Count: 1   +   2   +   3   +   4   +

DON'T PRACTICE THIS!

DAY 3: Yellow Bird

Key of _____ Major

What two L.H. chords are used?
Plan the opening rhythm.

Count: 1   +   2   +   3   + 4 +

15

DAY 4: Yellow Bird

Key of _____ Major

Draw an X through each **incorrect** measure. There are two.

16

Fill the blank measure with your **own 4/4 rhythm**.

DAY 5: Yellow Bird

Key of _____ Major

17

Circle the correct **key signatures** in F. There are two.

DAY 1: Morning

Key of _____ Major

Silently play the R.H. for measures 1-2. Notice the crossover.

DON'T PRACTICE THIS!

DAY 2: Morning

Key of _____ Major

DON'T PRACTICE THIS!

Scan the music. Notice this piece uses imitation between the hands.

Circle the correct **imitations** for the pattern. There are two.

PATTERN

19

DAY 3: Morning
Key of _____ Major
(for L.H. alone)

DON'T PRACTICE THIS!

Notice the key signature!

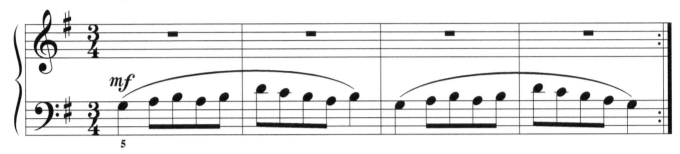

DAY 4: Morning
Key of _____ Major

Silently finger both L.H. chords before playing.

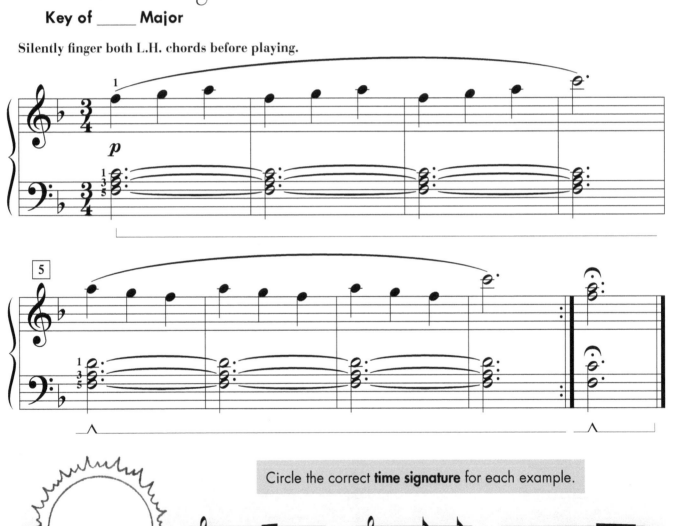

Circle the correct **time signature** for each example.

CONGRATULATIONS

DAY 5: Morning

Key of ____ Major

DON'T
PRACTICE
THIS!

Silently finger the R.H. for the last three measures.

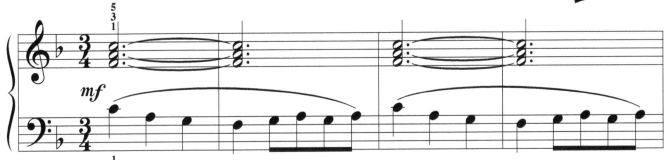

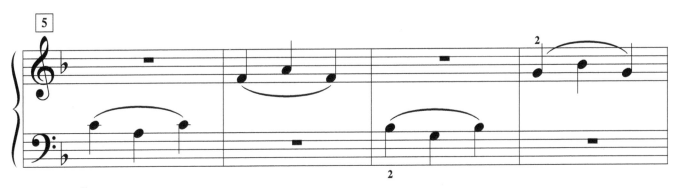

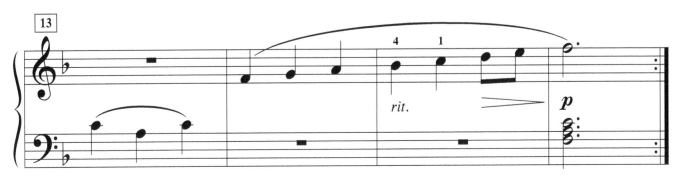

21

Circle all the intervals of a **7th**. There are three.

DAY 1: Land of the Silver Birch

Key of D Minor

DON'T PRACTICE **THIS!**

Name the opening L.H. interval. Scan the last line for the L.H. before playing.

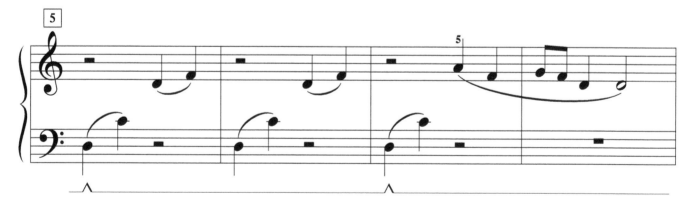

DAY 2: Land of the Silver Birch

Key of D Minor

DON'T PRACTICE THIS!

Notice the L.H. interval pattern in measures 1-2. Where does it repeat?

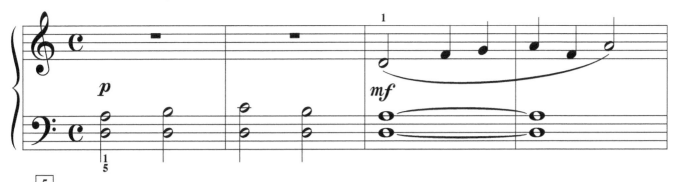

DAY 3: Land of the Silver Birch

Key of C Minor

Mentally hear the rhythm of the last two measures before playing.

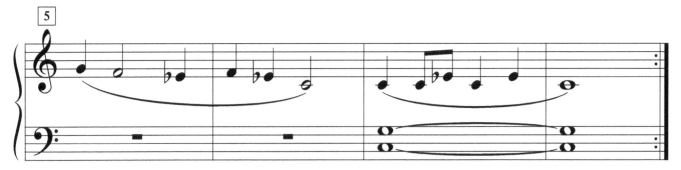

DAY 4: Land of the Silver Birch

Key of D Minor

DON'T PRACTICE THIS!

Silently finger the L.H. intervals. Notice how the thumb moves lower for each one.
Prepare your foot on the pedal.

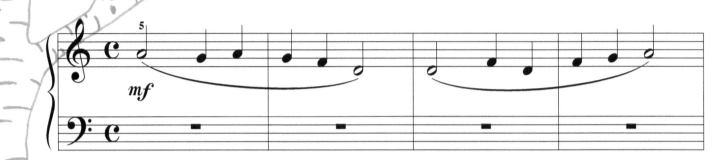

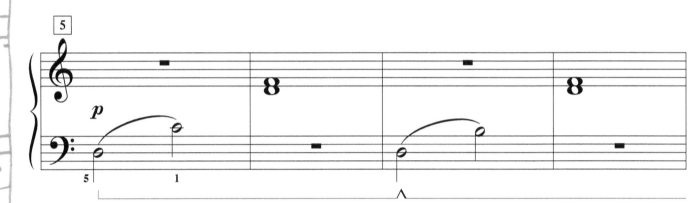

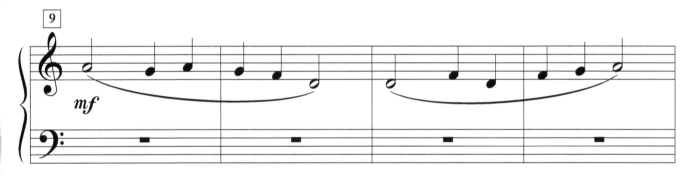

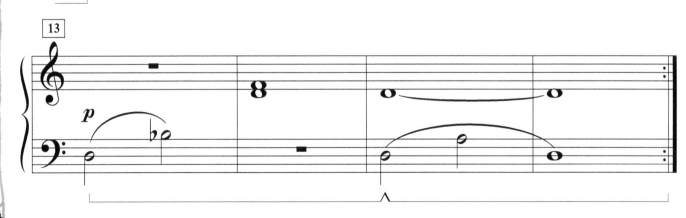

Complete each measure with a **rest:**

DAY 5: Land of the Silver Birch
Key of D Minor

DON'T PRACTICE **THIS!**

What is the opening L.H. interval? Notice the dynamics!

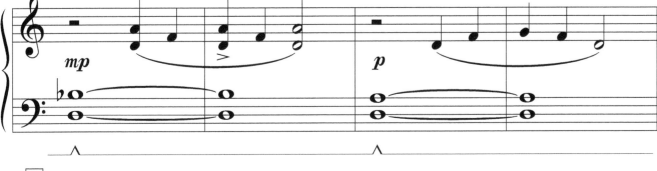

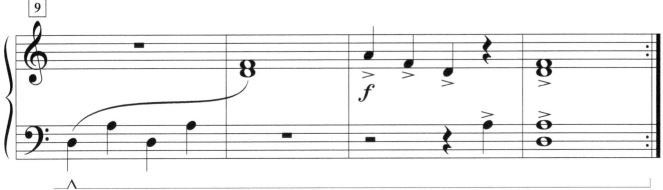

RHYTHM ROAD

Draw **bar lines** to match the time signature.

DAY 1: Cossack Ride

Key of A Minor

DON'T PRACTICE THIS!

Notice the L.H. 5ths shift at measures 5-6.
Mentally hear the rhythm for measures 1-2 before playing.

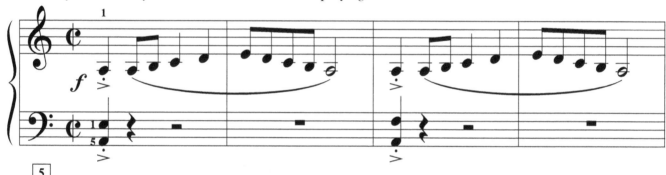

DAY 2: Cossack Ride

Key of D Minor

Notice the L.H. 5ths shift at measure 3.

DAY 3: Cossack Ride

Key of D Minor

Remember, a ♩. is often followed by a single ♪ note. Feel the dot on beat 2.

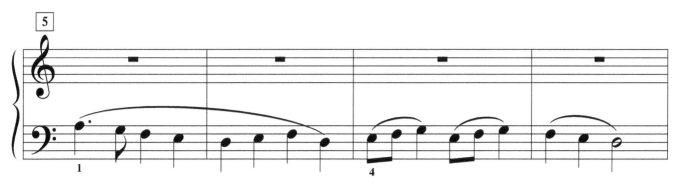

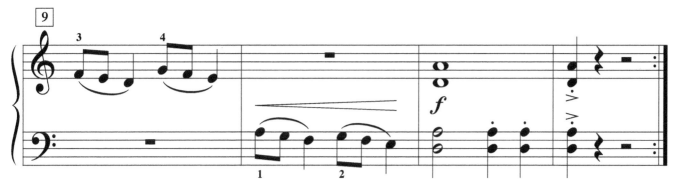

Write your own rhythm in **cut time**. You may refer to rhythm patterns in DAY 3 or DAY 4.

(you write)

DAY 4: Cossack Ride

Key of A Minor

Hint: Be sure to count the rests at measures 7-8.

Draw the correct clef to form the **A minor 5-finger scale**.

DAY 5: Cossack Ride

Key of A Minor

Scan the music, noticing the interval changes.

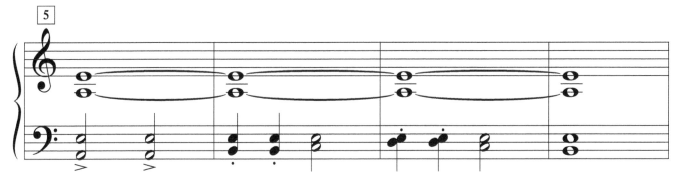

DAY 1: Lunar Eclipse

Key of C Minor

DON'T PRACTICE THIS!

Plan how you will play the last line of music.

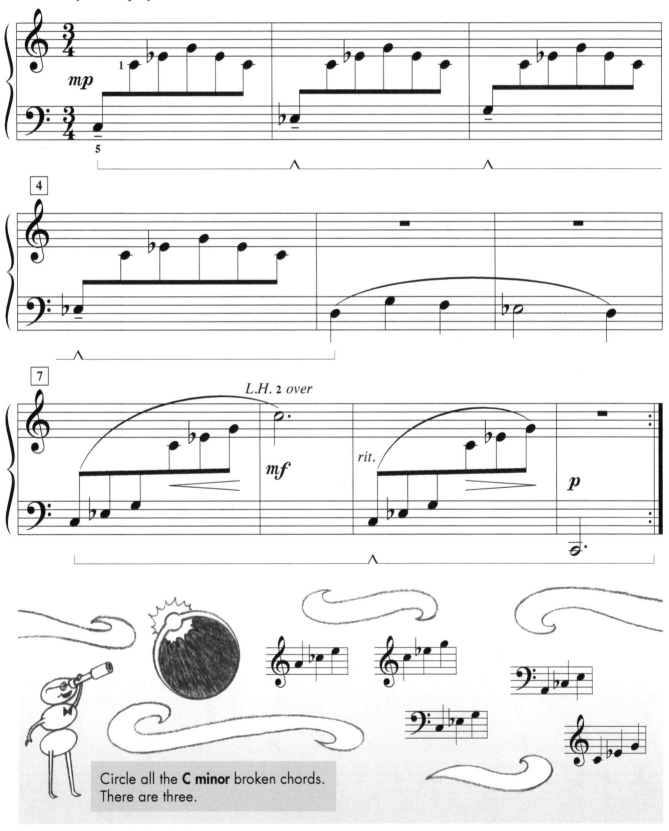

Circle all the **C minor** broken chords.
There are three.

30

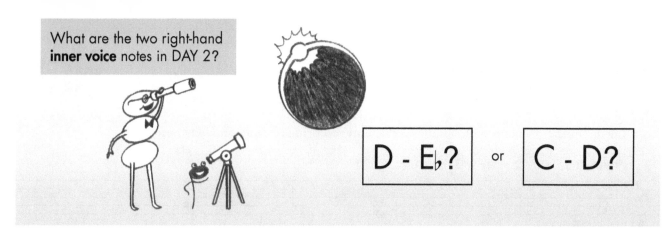

What are the two right-hand **inner voice** notes in DAY 2?

D - E♭? or C - D?

DAY 2: Lunar Eclipse

Key of C Minor

DON'T PRACTICE THIS!

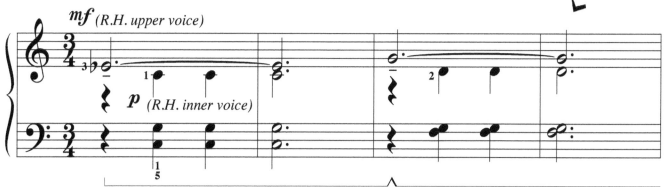

DAY 3: Lunar Eclipse

Key of G Minor

DAY 4: Lunar Eclipse

Key of C Minor

DON'T PRACTICE THIS!

Scan the opening R.H. notes with tenuto marks. Can you bring out these melody notes?

DAY 5: Lunar Eclipse

Key of C Minor

Scan the music. Where does the R.H. thumb shift to play a 6th?

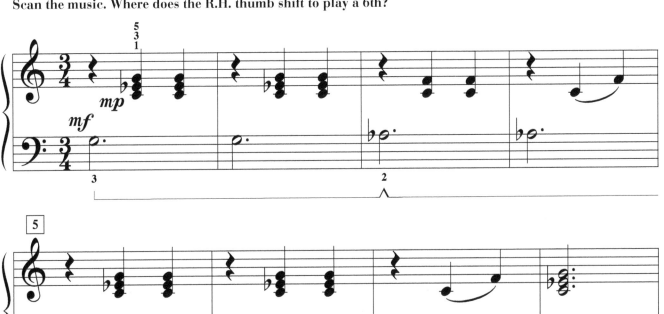

Congratulations, sightreader! Draw **bar lines** for this 3/4 rhythm.

DAY 1: Scarborough Fair
Key of D Minor

Circle all the **3/8 patterns** used in Scarborough Fair. There are three.

DAY 2: Scarborough Fair

Key of D Minor
(for L.H. alone)

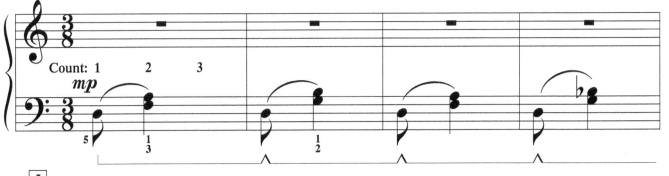

Count: 1   2   3

DAY 3: Scarborough Fair

Key of D Minor

Prepare the L.H. and the damper pedal before starting.

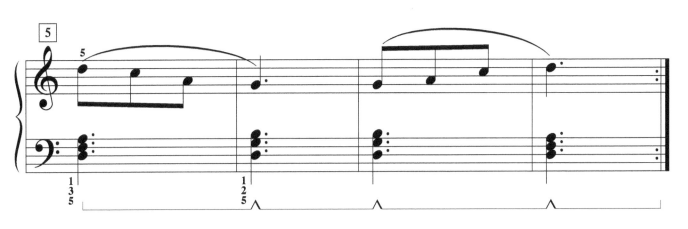

DAY 4: Scarborough Fair

Key of D Minor
(for L.H. alone)

Mentally hear the rhythm pattern in the second line before playing.
Notice the hand shift at measure 14.

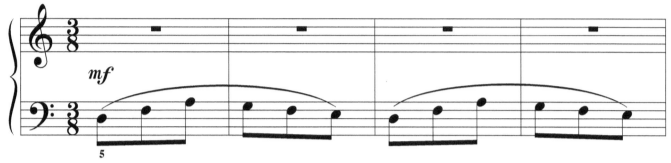

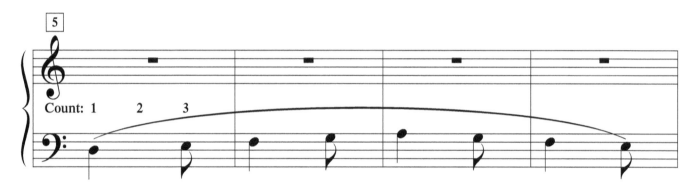

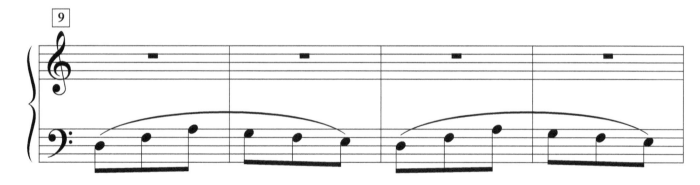

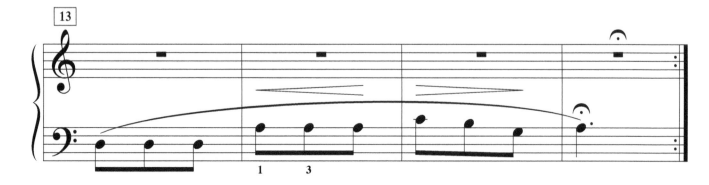

DAY 5: Scarborough Fair
Key of D Minor

DON'T PRACTICE THIS!

Mentally hear the rhythm of measures 1-2 before playing.

Congratulations! Now write 1 2 3 under the **correct beats**.

DAY 1: Night of the Tarantella
Key of A Minor

Count: 1 2 3 4 5 6

RHYTHM ROAD

Draw an X through the **incorrect** measures in 6/8 time. There are two.

Circle the **most common** 6/8 rhythm pattern in DAY 2.

DAY 2: Night of the Tarantella

Key of A Minor

DON'T PRACTICE THIS!

39

DAY 3: Night of the Tarantella
Key of A Minor

Remember, in fast tempos, 6/8 is felt with two big beats per measure.
Mentally hear the rhythm of measures 1-2 before playing.

DAY 4: Night of the Tarantella
Key of A Minor

Scan the music. Notice that the R.H. broken chords shift down the keys: Am, G, F, then E.
Silently finger these chords before sightreading.

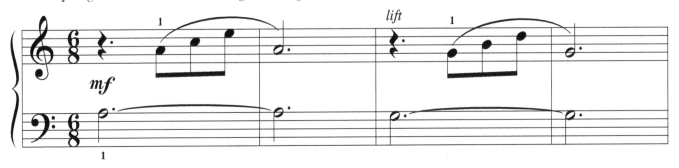

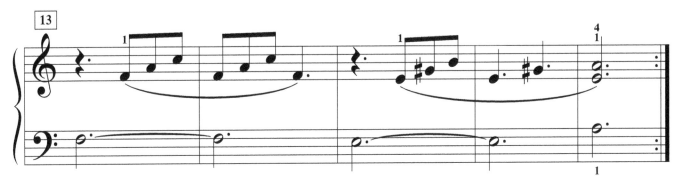

DAY 5: Night of the Tarantella
Key of A Minor

Write one **note** or **rest** to complete each measure:

CONGRATULATIONS DAY 5!

DAY 1: Candles and Cake

Key of _____ Major

DON'T PRACTICE THIS!

Notice the echo at measure 3 and measure 7.

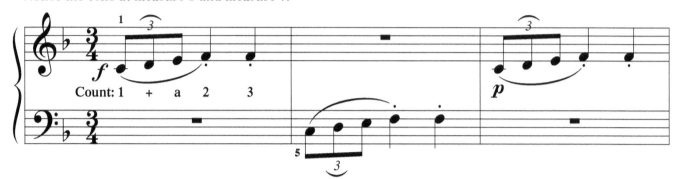

Count: 1   +   a   2   3

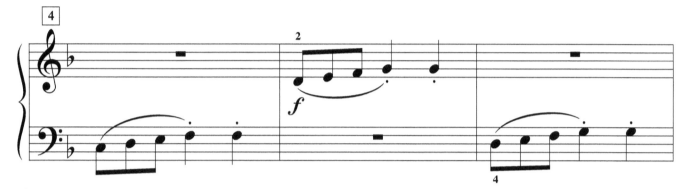

Complete each unfinished measure on the cake. Use at least one **triplet**.

Connect the layers of the cakes with the **same number** of beats.

DAY 2: Candles and Cake

Key of _____ Major

Mentally hear the first measure before playing.

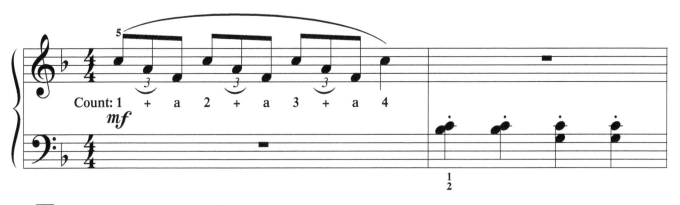

Count: 1 + a 2 + a 3 + a 4

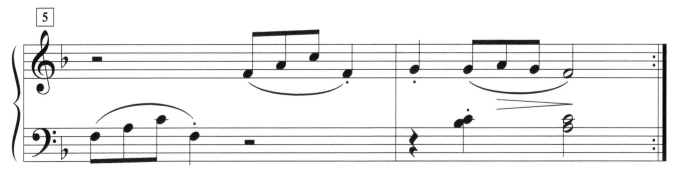

45

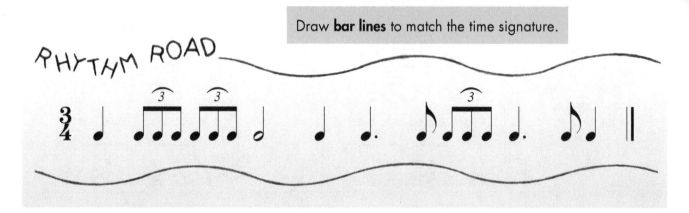

DAY 3: Candles and Cake

Key of _____ Major
(for L.H. alone)

DON'T PRACTICE THIS!

Scan the music for I, IV, and V7 chords before playing.

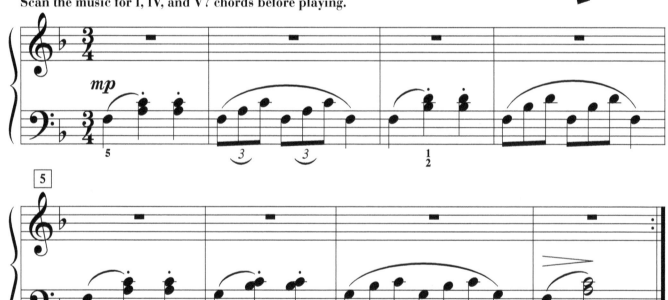

DAY 4: Candles and Cake

Key of _____ Major
(for L.H. alone)

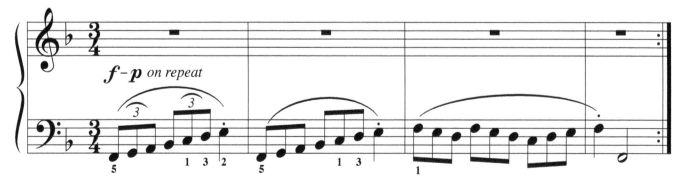

DAY 5: Candles and Cake

Key of _____ Major

Scan the music for I and IV chords.

DAY 1: Amazing Grace

Key of _____ Major

Connect each note to the matching number of **triplets**.

DAY 2: Amazing Grace

Key of _____ Major

DAY 3: Amazing Grace

Key of _____ Major

Silently finger the R.H. chords before playing.

49

DAY 4: Amazing Grace

Key of _____ Major

Complete these measures of rhythm. Use at least one **triplet** in each measure.

RHYTHM ROAD

50

DAY 5: Amazing Grace

Key of _____ Major

Notice that the R.H. shifts in measure 1.

Congratulations, Amazing Sightreader!

DAY 1: March Slav

Key of A Minor

Silently play the L.H. notes in the last measure before sightreading.

DAY 2: March Slav

Key of A Minor
(for L.H. alone)

Write the **letter names** of these bass ledger notes.
Then name the **interval**.

notes: __ __   notes: __ __   notes: __ __

interval: ____   interval: ____   interval: ____

DAY 3: March Slav

Key of A Minor

DON'T PRACTICE THIS!

DAY 4: March Slav

Key of A Minor

Mentally hear the rhythm of measure 4 before playing.

Congratulations! Write the following letter names as **bass ledger line** notes. Use whole notes.

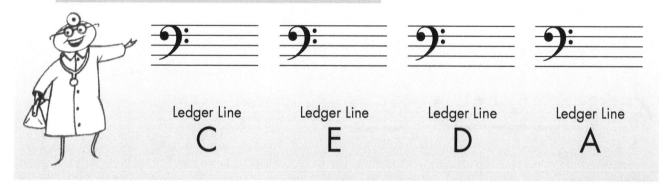

Ledger Line
C

Ledger Line
E

Ledger Line
D

Ledger Line
A

DAY 5: March Slav

Key of A Minor

DON'T
PRACTICE
THIS!

DAY 1: Cool Walkin' Bass

Key of _____ Major

Swing the 8th notes in a long-short pattern.

Connect the **letter names** to the correct notes.

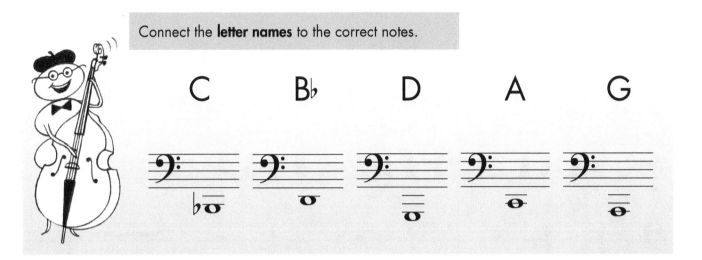

C   Bb   D   A   G

DAY 2: Cool Walkin' Bass

Key of _____ Major
(for L.H. alone)

> DON'T PRACTICE THIS!

Notice the 8va sign in the last measure.

57

DAY 3: Cool Walkin' Bass

Key of _____ Major

DON'T PRACTICE THIS!

Swing the 8th notes in a long-short pattern.

DAY 4: Cool Walkin' Bass

Key of _____ Major

DAY 5: Cool Walkin' Bass

Key of _____ Major

DON'T
PRACTICE
THIS!

Notice the key signature!

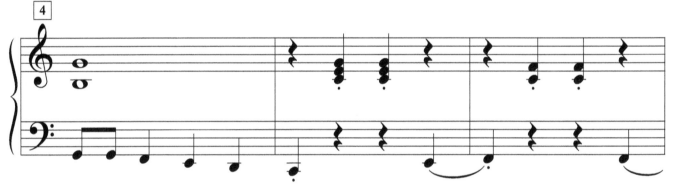

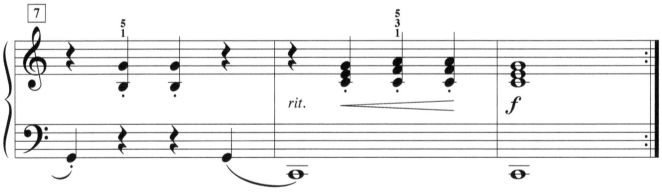

CONGRATULATIONS!

DAY 1: Joshua Fought the Battle of Jericho
Key of A Minor

DON'T PRACTICE THIS!

Swing the 8th notes in a long-short pattern.

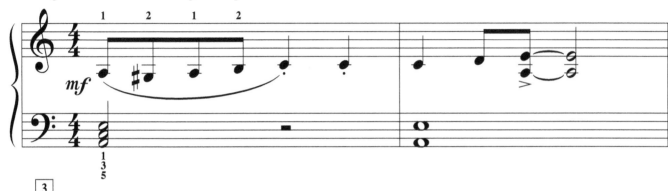

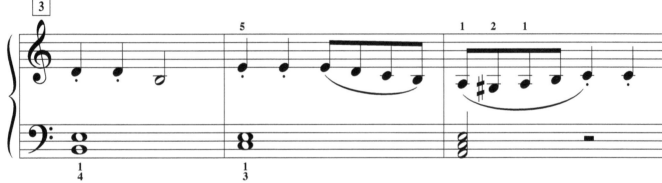

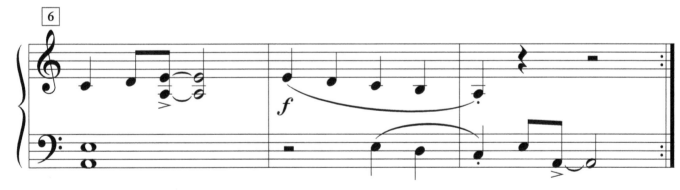

Name these **inner** ledger line notes.

Name these **intervals** (2nd, 3rd, 4th, 5th, 6th, or 7th).

DAY 2: Joshua Fought the Battle of Jericho
Key of A Minor

DON'T
PRACTICE
THIS!

DAY 3: Joshua Fought the Battle of Jericho
Key of A Minor

 DON'T PRACTICE THIS!

DAY 4: Joshua Fought the Battle of Jericho
Key of A Minor
(for L.H. alone)

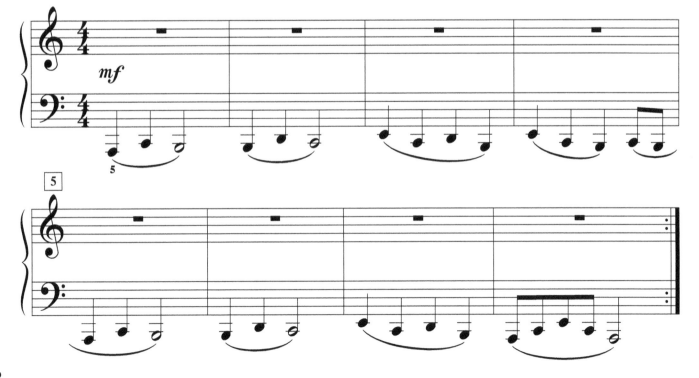

Complete each measure by writing **one or more** notes.

RHYTHM ROAD

DAY 5: Joshua Fought the Battle of Jericho
Key of A Minor

Swing the 8th notes in a long-short pattern.

63

DAY 1: The Great Wall of China

Key of _____ Major

DON'T PRACTICE THIS!

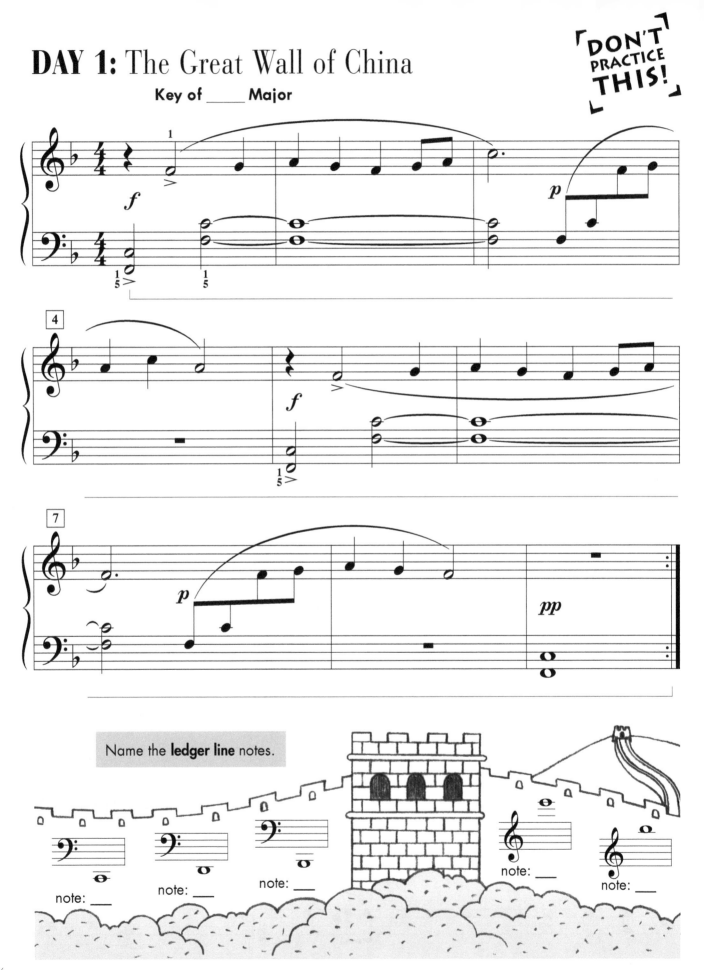

Name the **ledger line** notes.

note: ___ note: ___ note: ___ note: ___ note: ___

64

DAY 2: The Great Wall of China

Key of _____ Major

Notice the shifts for the left hand. Silently finger them before playing.

DAY 3: The Great Wall of China

Drape your fingers over the black keys before playing.

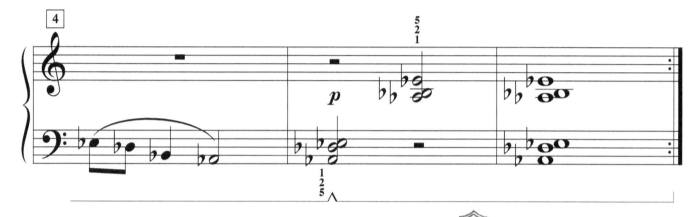

DAY 4: The Great Wall of China

Key of _____ Minor

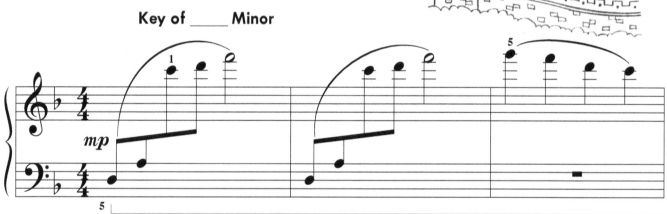

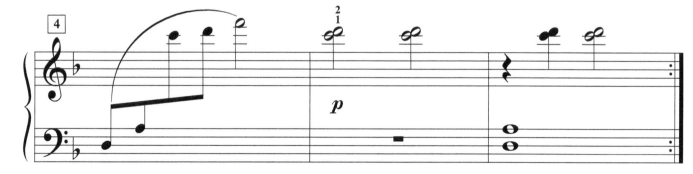

DAY 5: The Great Wall of China

Key of _____ Major
(for L.H. alone)

DON'T PRACTICE THIS!

DAY 5! CONGRATULATIONS, SIGHTREADER!

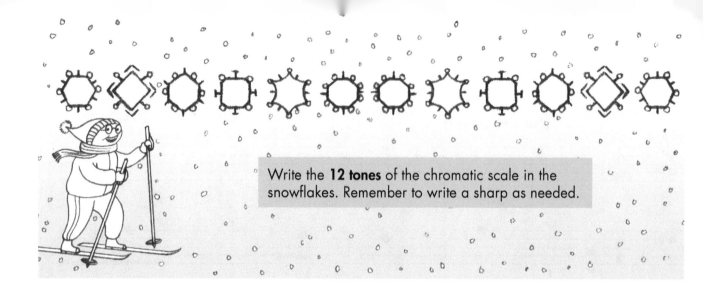

Write the **12 tones** of the chromatic scale in the snowflakes. Remember to write a sharp as needed.

DAY 1: Snowflake Rag

Key of _____ Major

DON'T PRACTICE THIS!

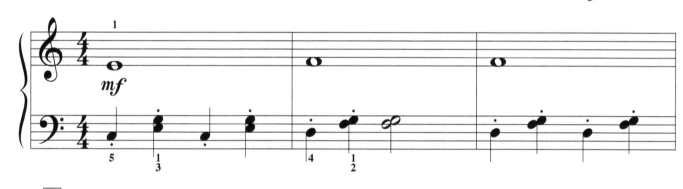

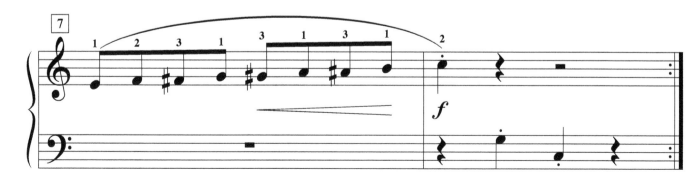

DAY 2: Snowflake Rag

Key of _____ Major

DON'T PRACTICE THIS!

Silently finger the L.H. chromatic passage at measures 3-4.

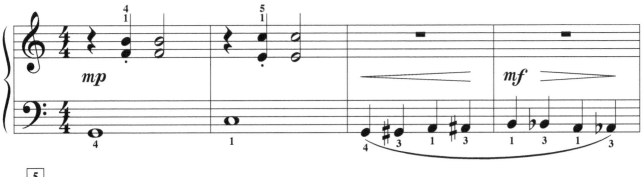

Circle each snowflake that is **chromatic** (only half steps).
There are three.

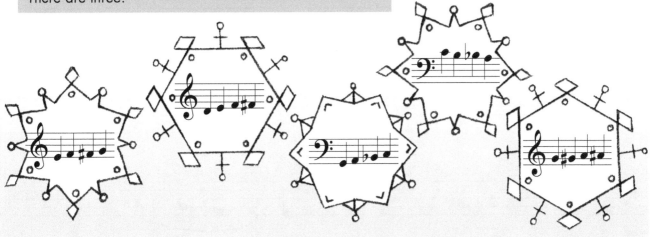

69

DAY 3: Snowflake Rag

DON'T PRACTICE THIS!

DAY 4: Snowflake Rag

Key of _____ Major

Complete these **chromatic** examples by filling in the blanks.

F# ___ ___ ___ ___ B

B ___ ___ ___ E

G# ___ ___ ___ ___ C#

DAY 5: Snowflake Rag

Key of _____ Major

DON'T PRACTICE THIS!

Plan how you will play the chromatic scale at measure 7.

71

DAY 1: Simple Gifts

Key of _____ Major

DON'T
PRACTICE
THIS!

Silently finger the crossover to C♯ in measure 1.

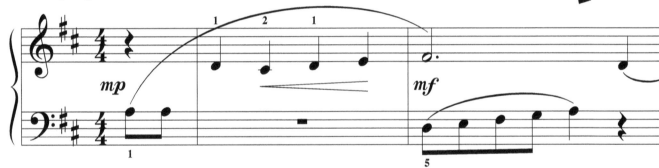

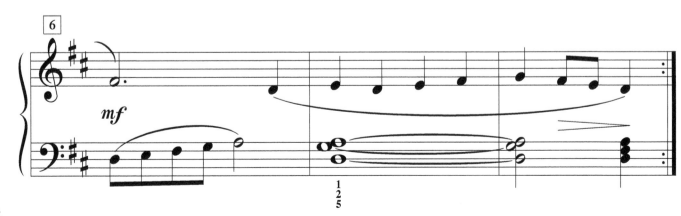

DAY 2: Simple Gifts

Key of _____ Major

Silently finger the R.H. intervals at measures 3-4. Where will you play a C♯?

Shade in the **sharped notes** for each D scale.

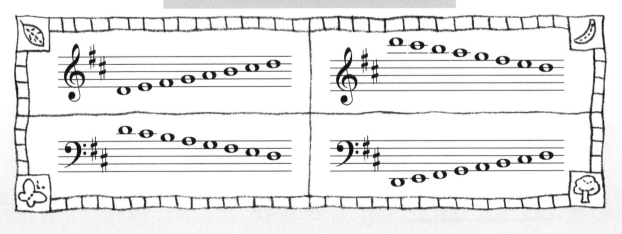

DAY 3: Simple Gifts

Key of _____ Major

Scan the music. Plan how you will play the crossovers for each scale.

DAY 4: Simple Gifts

Key of _____ Major

Rest your fingers on the D major keys so you are ready for the scale in contrary motion.

Name the **key signature** for each example in the quilt.

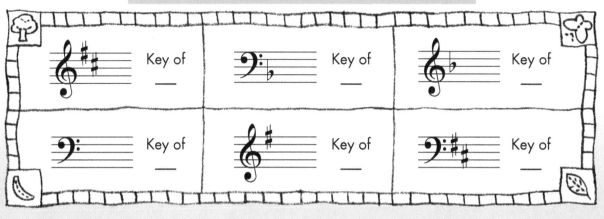

DAY 5: Simple Gifts

Key of _____ Major

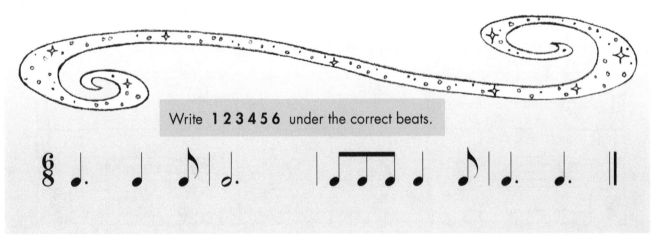

Write **1 2 3 4 5 6** under the correct beats.

DAY 1: Tchaikovsky's Theme

Key of _____ Major

DON'T PRACTICE THIS!

DAY 2: Tchaikovsky's Theme

Key of _____ Major

DON'T PRACTICE THIS!

Prepare your R.H. finger 4 over the C♯ before playing.

Write the **letter names** of the D major scale. Include any sharps.

Scale Degrees: D ___ ___ ___ ___ ___ ___ ___
              1   2   3   4   5   6   7 8(1)

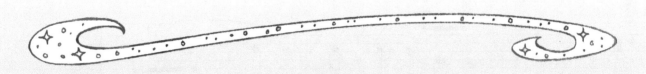

DAY 3: Tchaikovsky's Theme

Key of _____ Major

Silently finger the L.H. chords. Plan how you will play the last R.H. 6th. Is there a sharp?

DAY 4: Tchaikovsky's Theme

Key of _____ Major
(for L.H. alone)

Scan the music, noticing the finger substitutions in measures 2 and 5.

DAY 5: Tchaikovsky's Theme

Key of _____ Major

DON'T PRACTICE THIS!

Plan the hand shifts from measure 1 to 2.

DAY 1: Allegro in D Major

Label all the notes correctly in the key of D major:

T = tonic, 1st degree **D** = dominant, 5th degree **LT** = leading tone, 7th degree

DAY 2: Allegro in D Major
(for L.H. alone)

DON'T PRACTICE THIS!

Name these **intervals** in the D major scale.

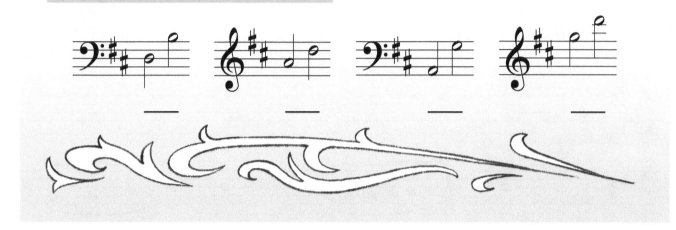

___   ___   ___   ___

DAY 3: Allegro in D Major

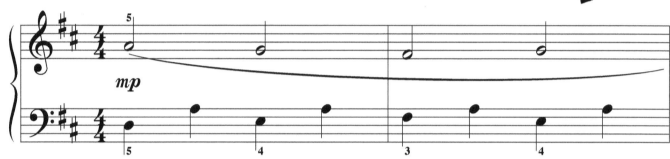

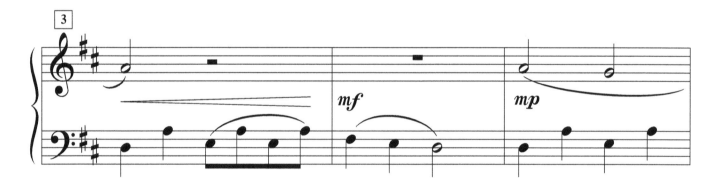

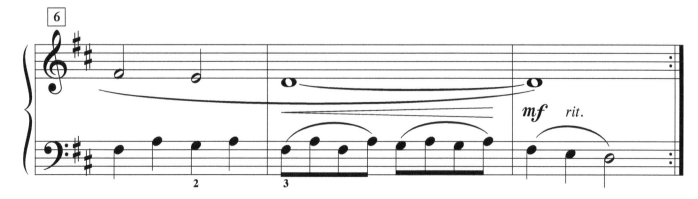

82

DAY 4: Allegro in D Major

Prepare R.H. finger 3 over the C♯ before playing.

DAY 5: Allegro in D Major

Complete the information for each example in **D major**.

Draw the D major
key signature.

Write I, IV, or V7 in each box
to show the **harmony**.

Draw a **D major scale**. Use whole notes.
Shade the sharped keys.

How has **sightreading**
helped your musicianship?

DAY 1: Novela

Key of A Minor

DON'T PRACTICE THIS!

Silently finger each L.H. one-octave arpeggio.

Name the **one-octave arpeggios** below. Circle major or minor.

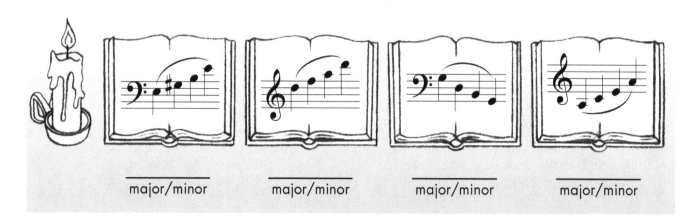

major/minor   major/minor   major/minor   major/minor

Circle the **correct spelling** for these one-octave arpeggios.

Cm	E	Dm	G
C - E - G - C	E - G# - B - E	D - A - F# - D	G - B♭ - D - G
C - E♭ - G - C	E - G - B - E	D - F - A - D	G - B - D - G

DAY 2: Novela

Key of A Minor

DON'T PRACTICE THIS!

DAY 3: Novela
Key of A Minor

Silently finger the R.H. one-octave arpeggios before playing.

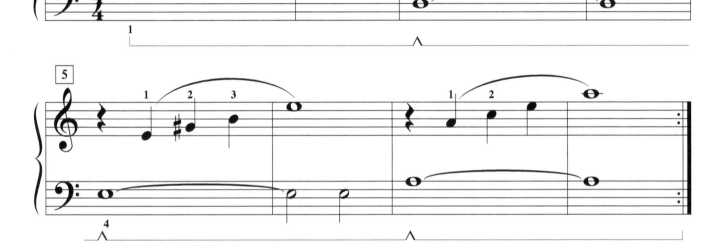

DAY 4: Novela
Key of C Major

Silently finger the L.H. one-octave arpeggios before playing. What chords are you playing?

DAY 5: Novela

Key of A Minor

DON'T PRACTICE THIS!

Silently finger the L.H. one-octave arpeggios. Find the final L.H. chord. Is it major or minor?

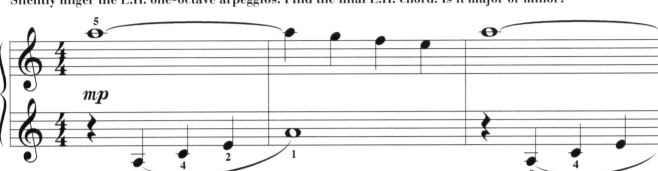

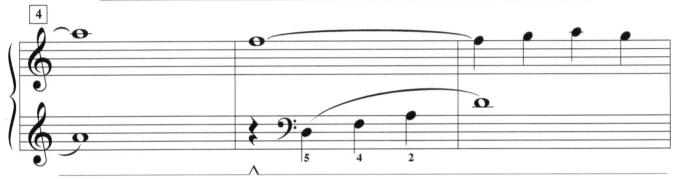

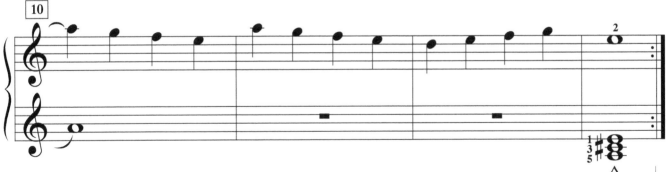

Congratulations!

Draw the **correct clef** and **key signature** to form the D major scale.

Draw ↓

Draw ↓

DAY 1: Willow Tree Waltz

Key of _____ Major

Silently finger the R.H. notes for the last line. Remember the C♯!

DON'T PRACTICE **THIS!**

90

DAY 2: Willow Tree Waltz

DON'T PRACTICE THIS!

Key of _____ Major

Is the opening measure of each line major or minor?

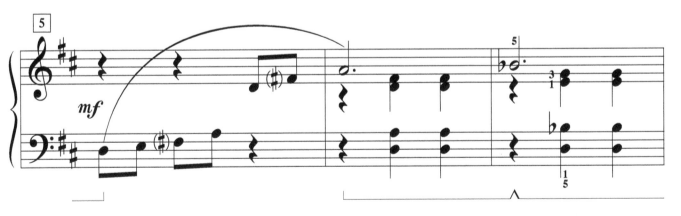

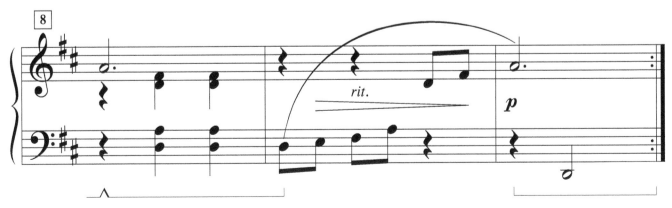

DAY 3: Willow Tree Waltz

Key of _____ Major
(for L.H. alone)

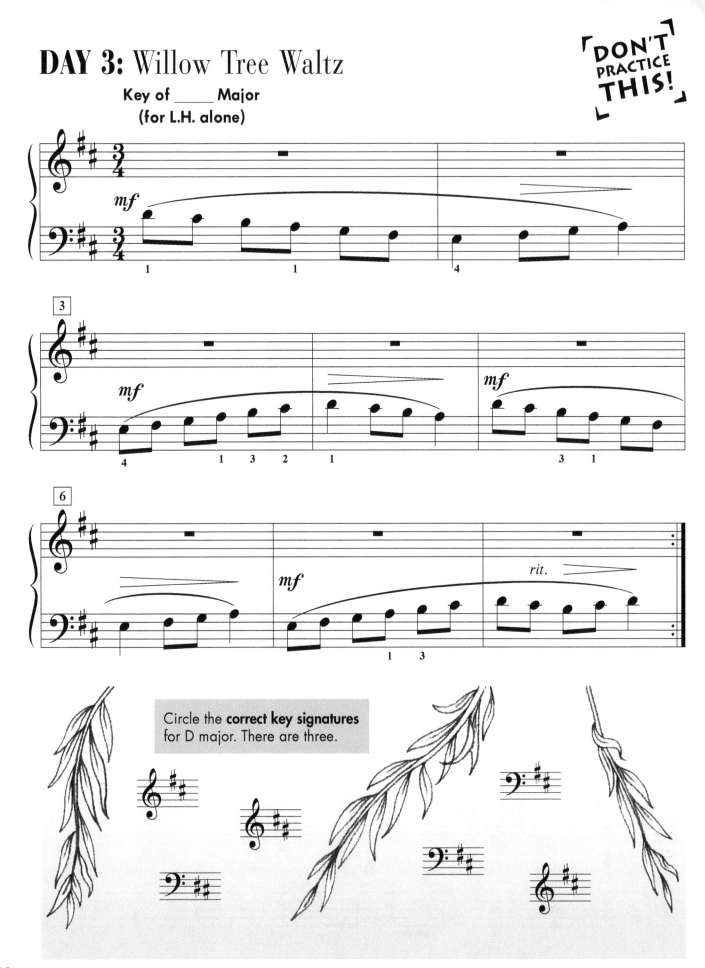

Circle the **correct key signatures** for D major. There are three.

DAY 4: Willow Tree Waltz

Key of _____ Major

Plan how you will play the last two measures.

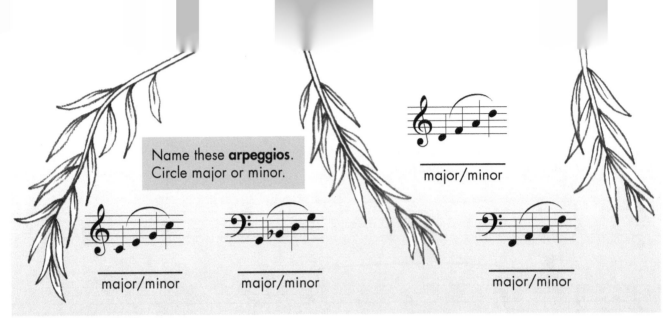

Name these **arpeggios**.
Circle major or minor.

major/minor

major/minor

major/minor

major/minor

DAY 5: Willow Tree Waltz

Key of _____ Major

DON'T
PRACTICE
THIS!

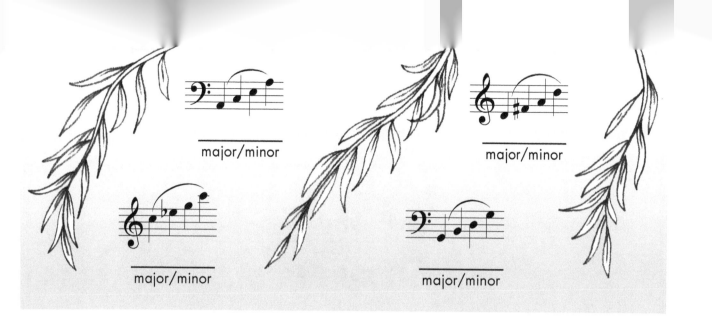

major/minor

major/minor

major/minor

major/minor

Piano Adventures® Certificate

CONGRATULATIONS

_____

(Your Name)

You are now a Level 3A Sightreader. Keep up the great work!

_____

Teacher

_____

Date